Wisconsin State Capitol

Madison

Jane Moorman

There is a saying, "It was a Friday night and it seemed like a good idea at the time." That sums up the beginning of the State Capitols Project.

When I told my brother of my idea of photographing state capitols, he said, "You do know there are 50 states and two of them you can't drive to."

Each capitol has its own unique beauty that reflects the state's personality when it was built.

Jane Moorman, photographer

Wisconsin: The badger State

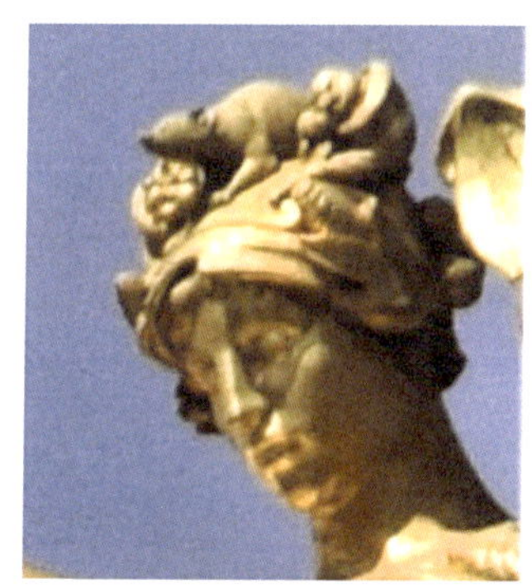

Wisconsin's uniqueness is the ever-present badger in various locations in the capitol, including on top of the Golden Lady's head, top photo.

The badger was designated the official state animal in 1957. It appears on the state flag, state seal and is even mentioned in the state song.

Wisconsin's nickname is "The Badger State" because miners dug tunnels into hillsides searching for lead ore in the 1800s and often lived in abandoned mine shafts, reminding people of badgers. The nickname also describes the hardworking, energetic settlers of the Wisconsin Territory.

The badger has also sailed at sea on the USS Wisconsin as a bronze plaque. In 1899, the state of Wisconsin presented the bronze badger, middle photo, to the US Navy for installation on the recently completed battleship USS Wisconsin.

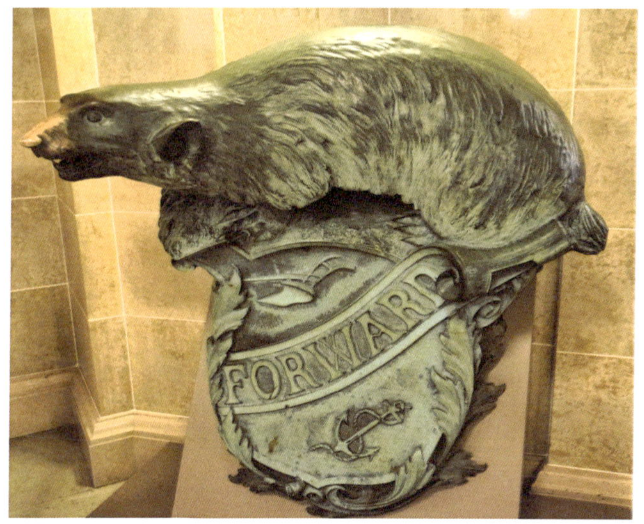

The plaque was designed by Milwaukee artist Paul Kupper and was cast with bronze salvage from Spanish cannons captured in Cuba during the Spanish-American War.

It is a symbol of the state pride and the spirit of cooperation between the state and the Navy. While aboard the ship, sailors rubbed the badger's nose for good luck. In 1988, plaque returned to the state historical society.

The badger also resides in the capitol, overlooking the entrance to the legislative chambers, bottom photo.

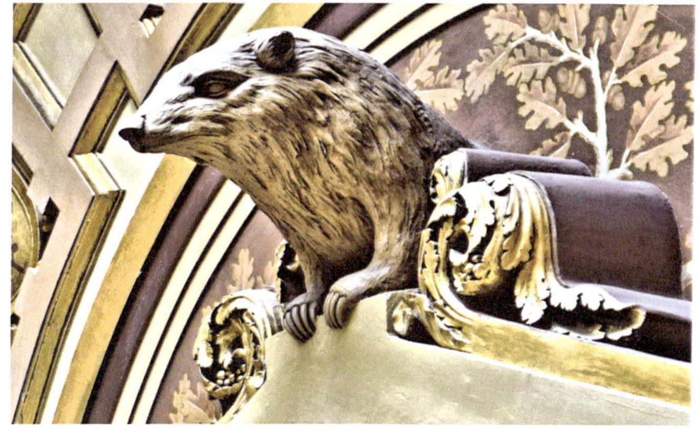

Golden Lady

The statue of Wisconsin on the top of the dome was produced by Daniel Chester French. It is often referred to as the "Golden Lady."

The statue is 15 feet and 4 inches tall, with a raised right hand pointing forward to signify the state's motto and a right hand holding a globe with an eagle perching atop it. Her helmet is famously crested by a badger.

French's other well-known statues include "Minute Man" in Concord, Massachusetts, and the massive, seated statue of Abraham Lincoln central to the Lincoln Memorial in Washington, D.C.

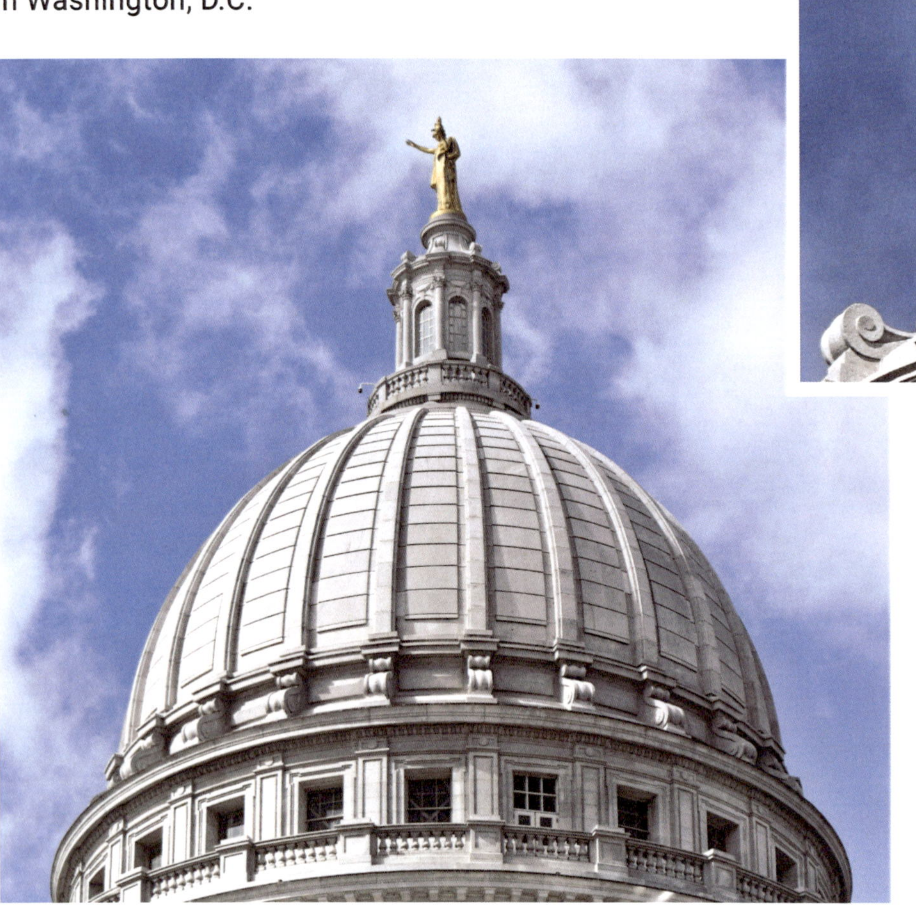

The Building

Construction of the present capitol, the third in Madison, began in late 1906 and was completed in 1917. The architects was George B. Post & Sons from New York.

The building is 284 feet, 5 inches tall from the ground floor to the top of the "Wisconsin" statue on the dome.

The capitol was constructed of 43 types of stone from six countries and eight states. The exterior stone is Bethel white granite from Vermont, making the exterior dome the largest granite dome in the world.

The corridor floors, walls and columns are of marble from the states of Tennessee, Missouri, Vermont, Georgia, New York, and Maryland; granite from the states of Wisconsin and Minnesota; and limestone from the states of Minnesota and Illinois. Marble from the countries of France, Italy, Greece, Algeria and Germany, and syenite from Norway are also present in the interior.

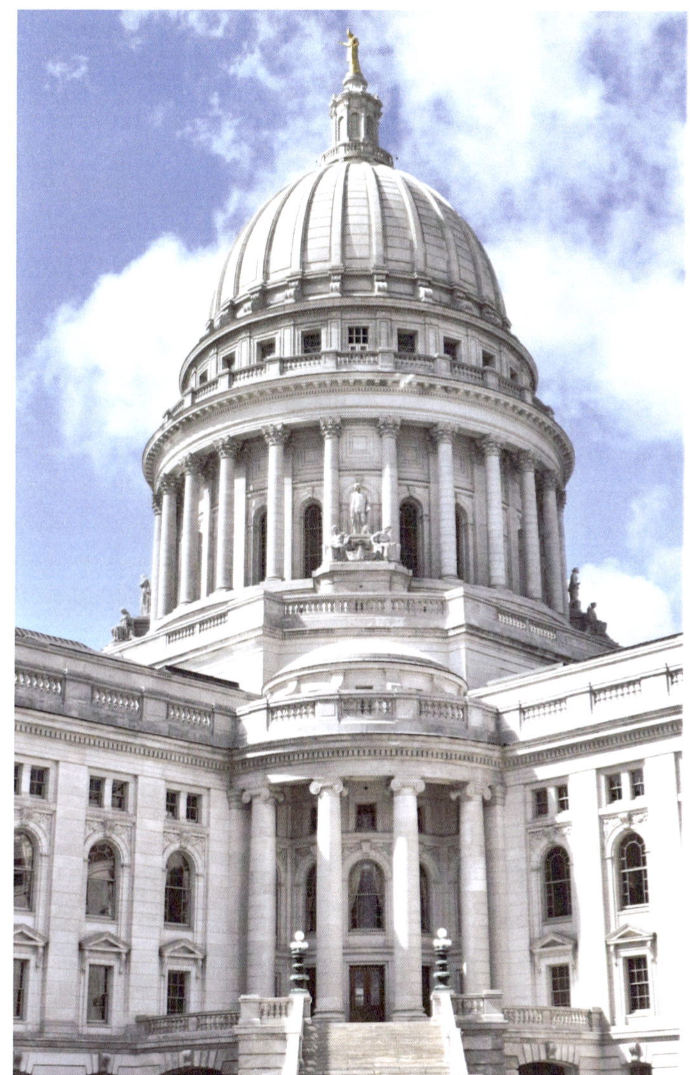

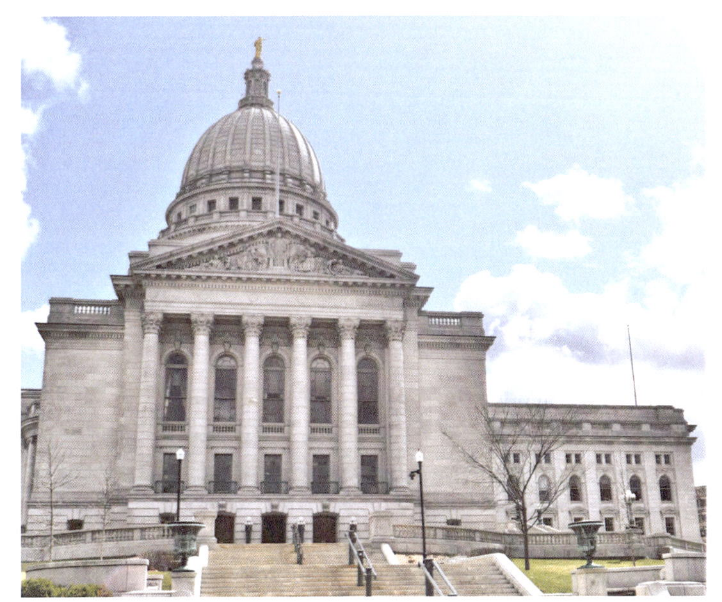

The capitol underwent a renovation project from 1988 to 2002. The purpose of the project was to convert the capitol into a modern working building, while restoring and preserving its original 1917 appearance.

Remodeling projects of the 1960s and 70s had introduced features out of character with the architecture of the building. Many original decorative stencils were painted over.

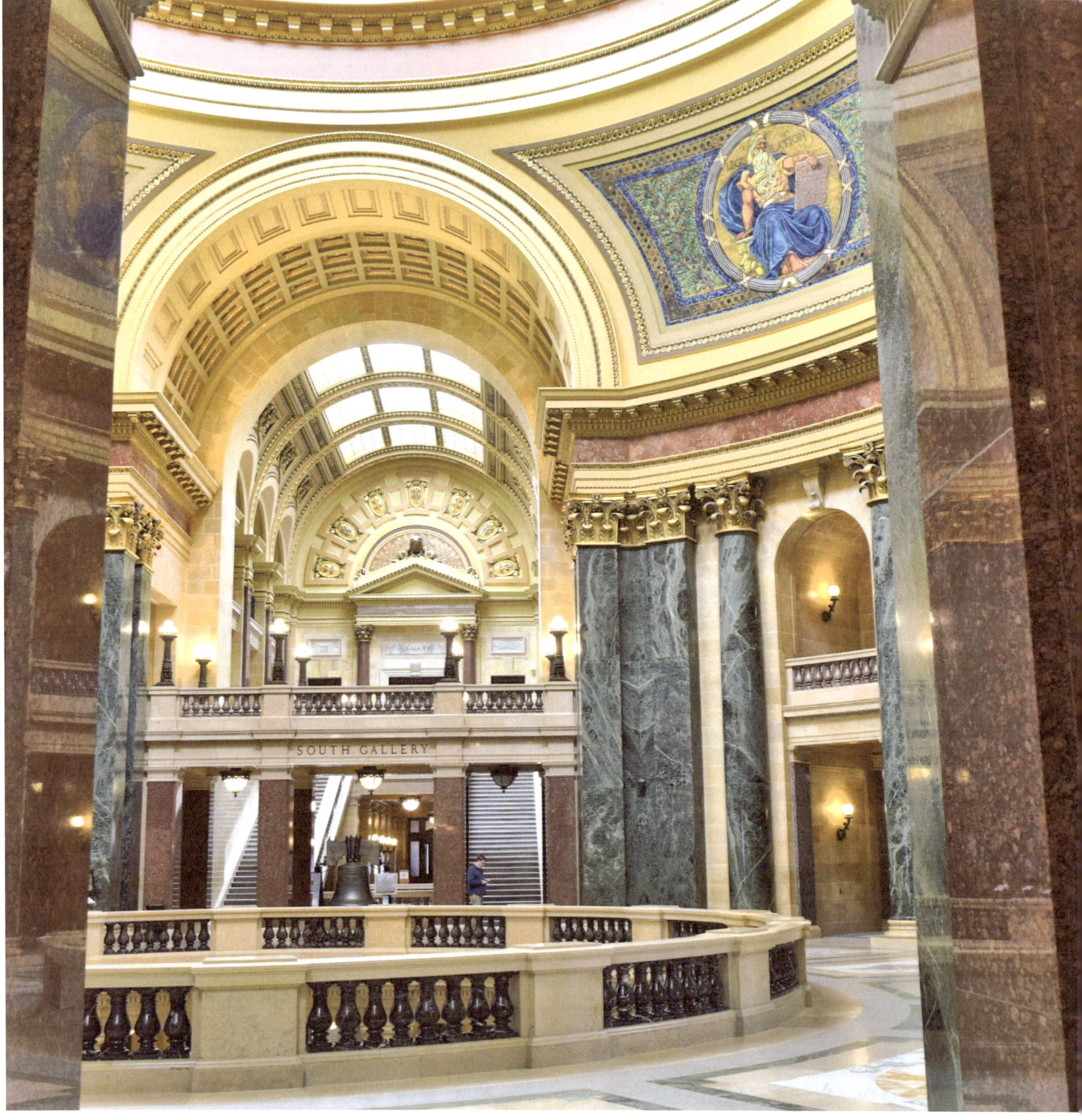

SOUTH GALLERY

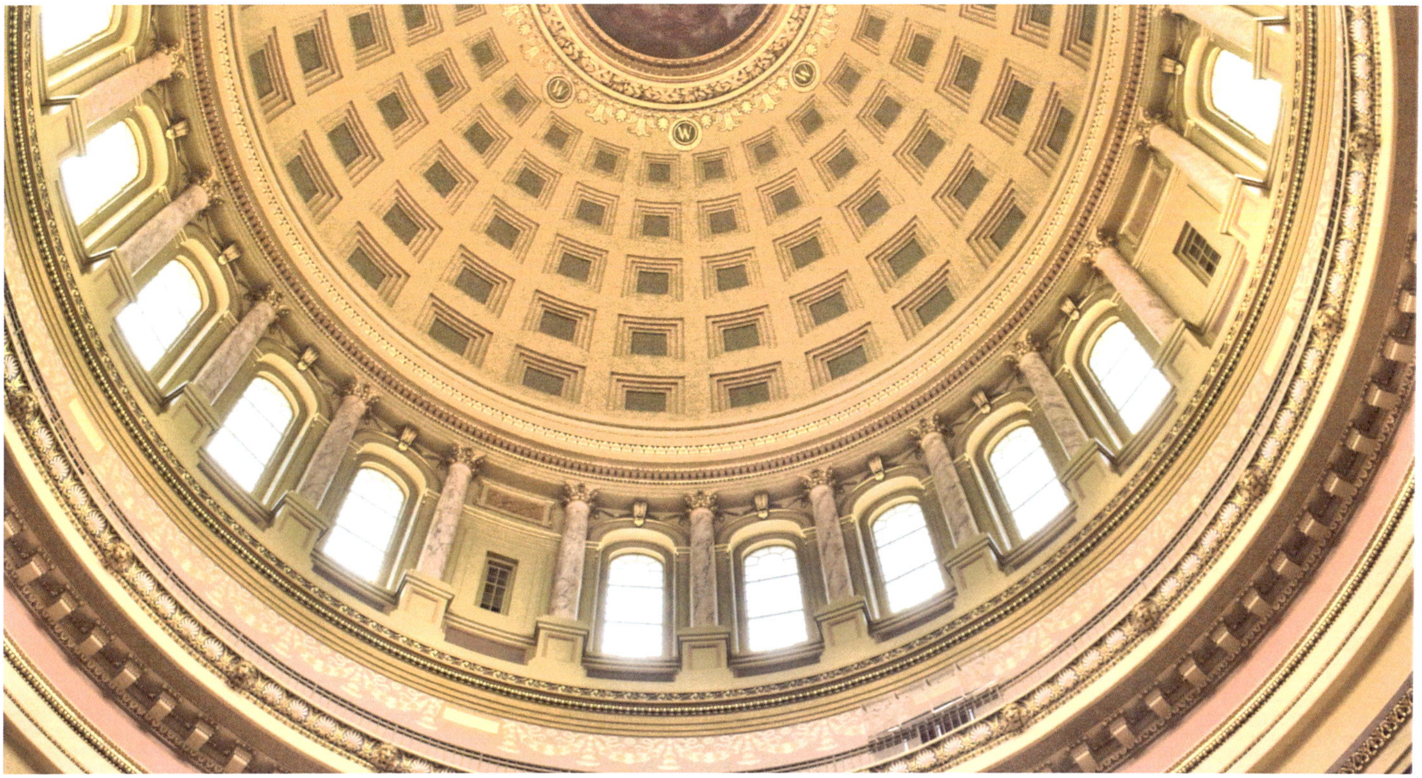

Rotunda Dome

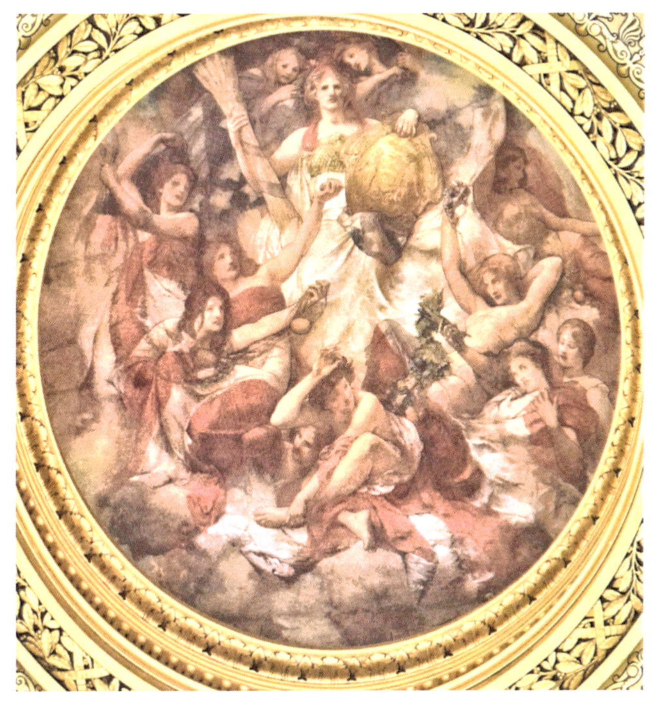

Edwin Blashfield created the painting that appears in the 34-foot diameter Capitol rotunda oculus.

Its subject is the resources of Wisconsin. The central figure is draped in an American flay and holding scepter of wheat. She is surrounded by companions holding other state products: lead, copper, tobacco, fruit, and a freshwater pearl.

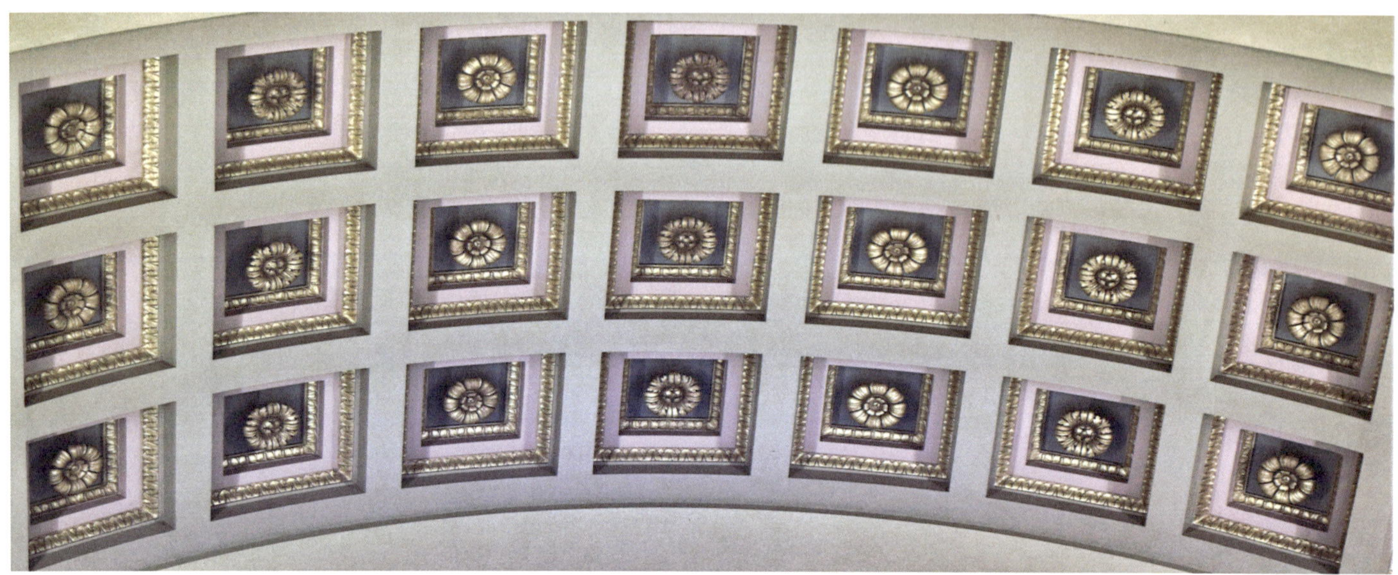

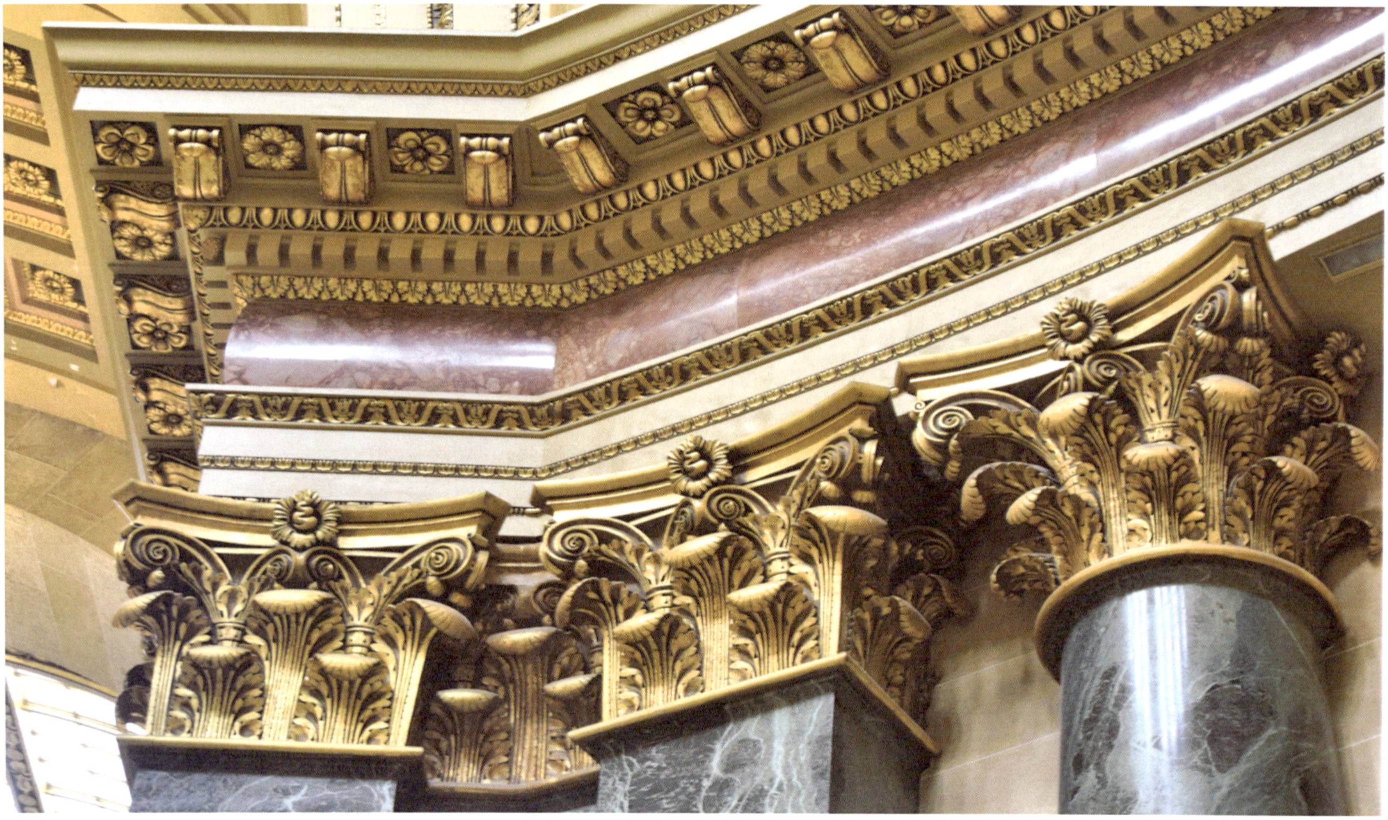

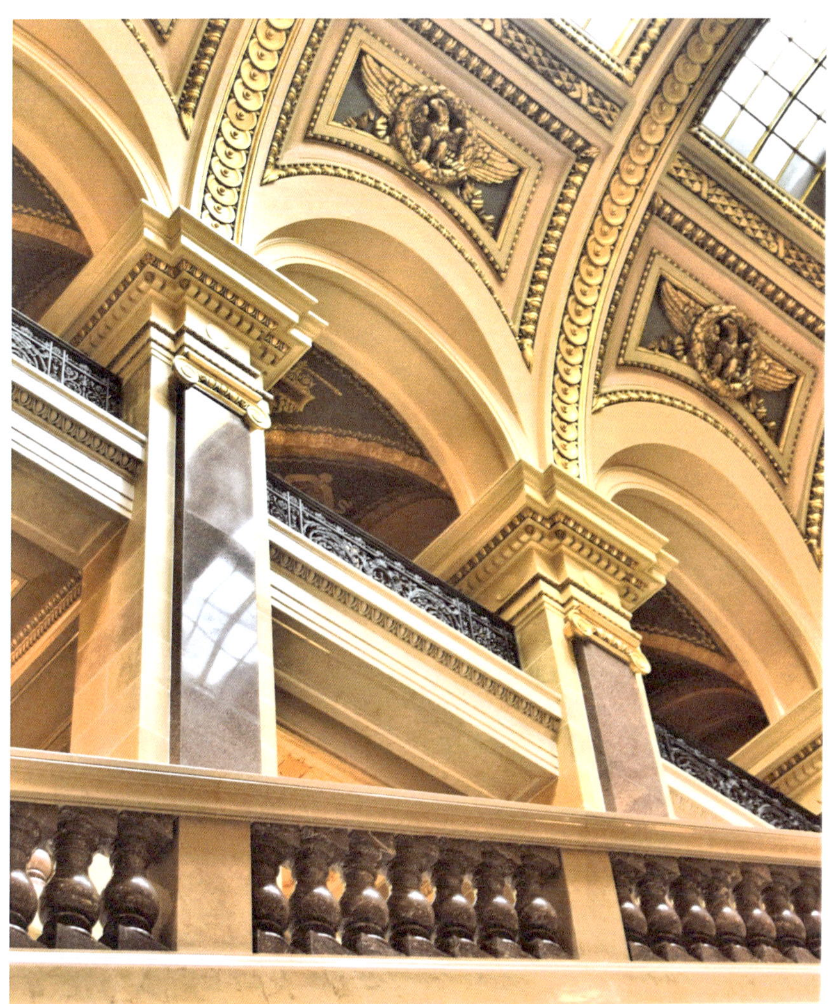
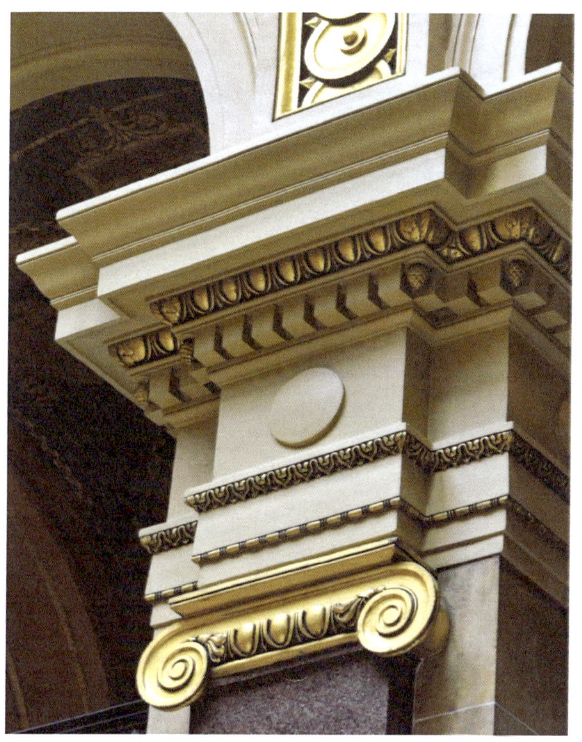
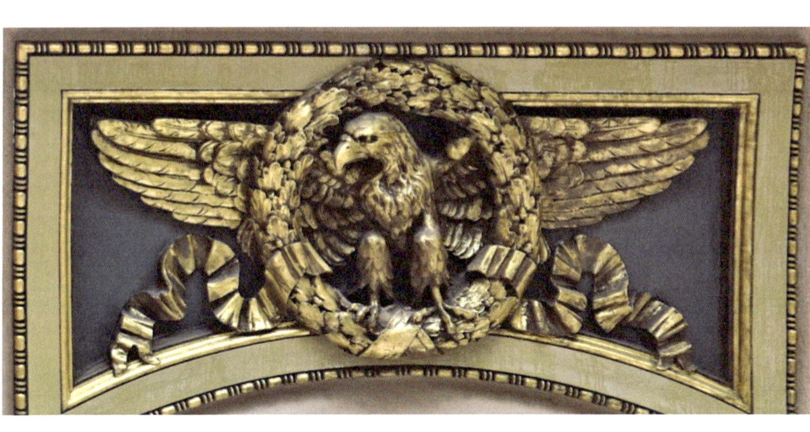
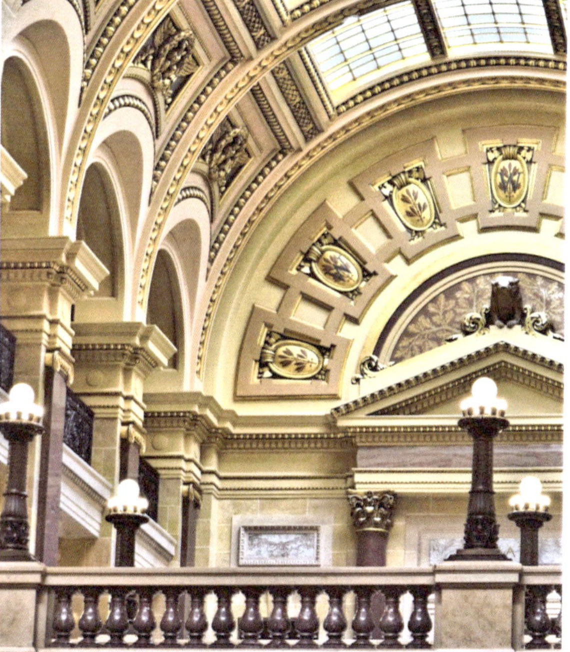

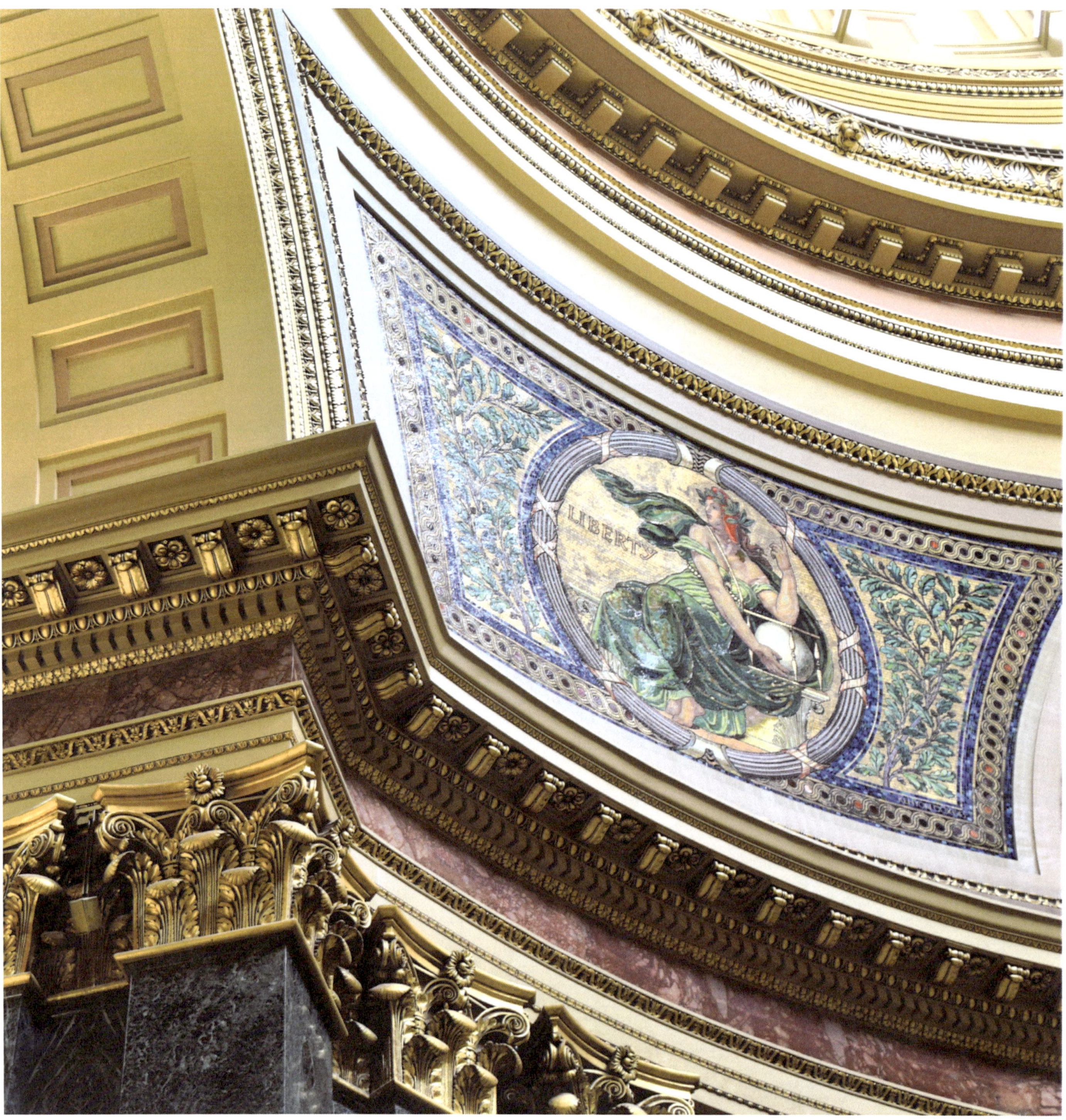
LIBERTY

Rotunda Glass Mosaics

Kenyan Cox created the four mosaics inside the capitol's rotunda.

Each mosaic is located at the pendentive, which is the structural feature in a building that transitions between a round dome and square building.

The mosaics represent the three branches of government and the people who empower them -- Legislation, Government, Justice and Liberty.

Each mosaic is about 12 feet high and 24 feet wide, and individually includes about 100,000 pieces of glass.

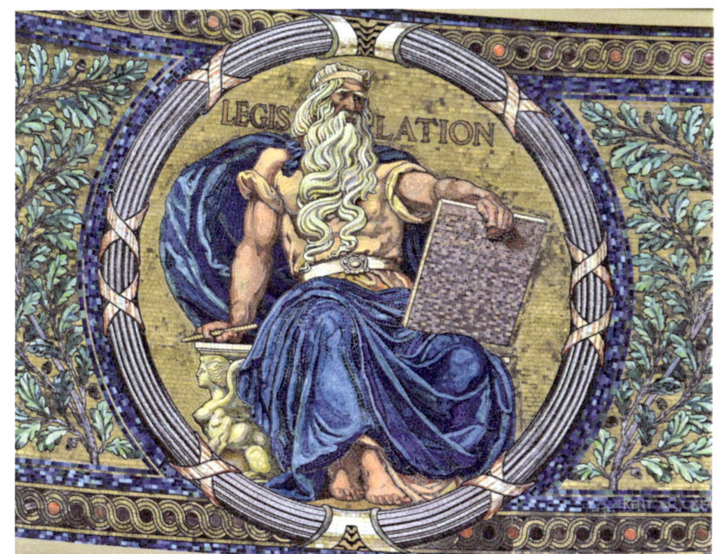

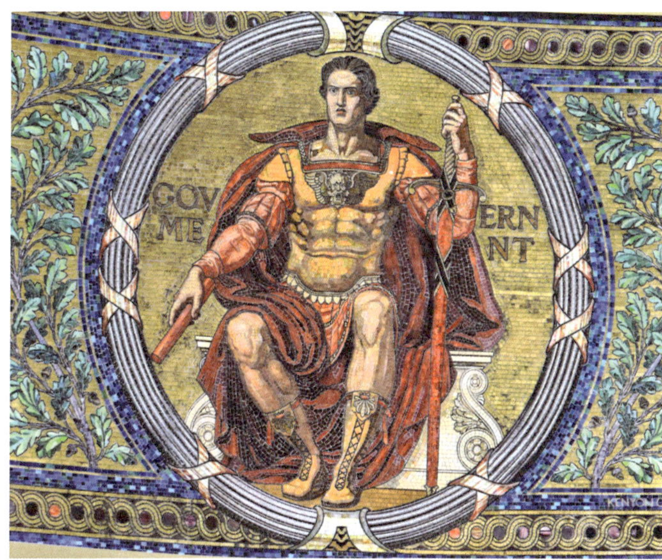

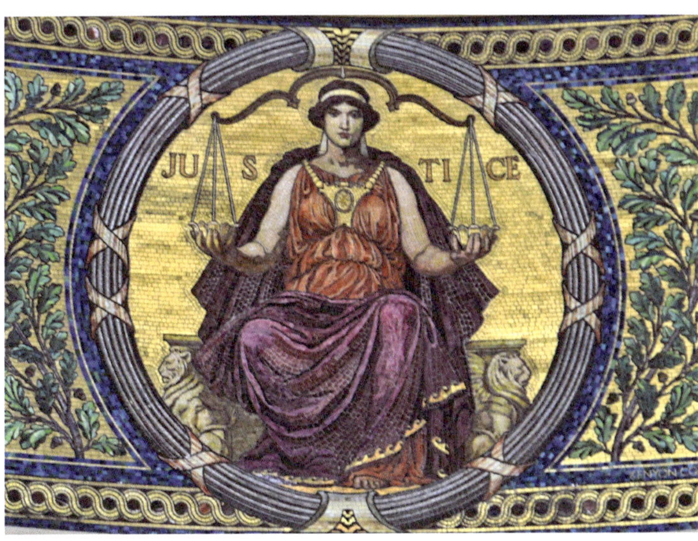

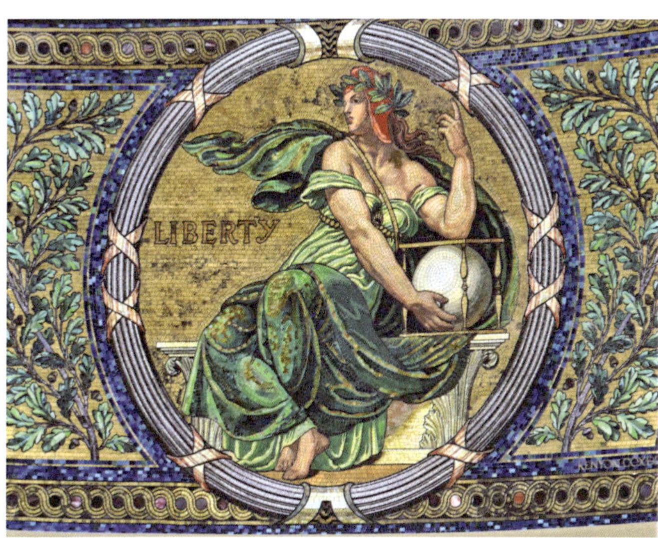

Senate Chamber

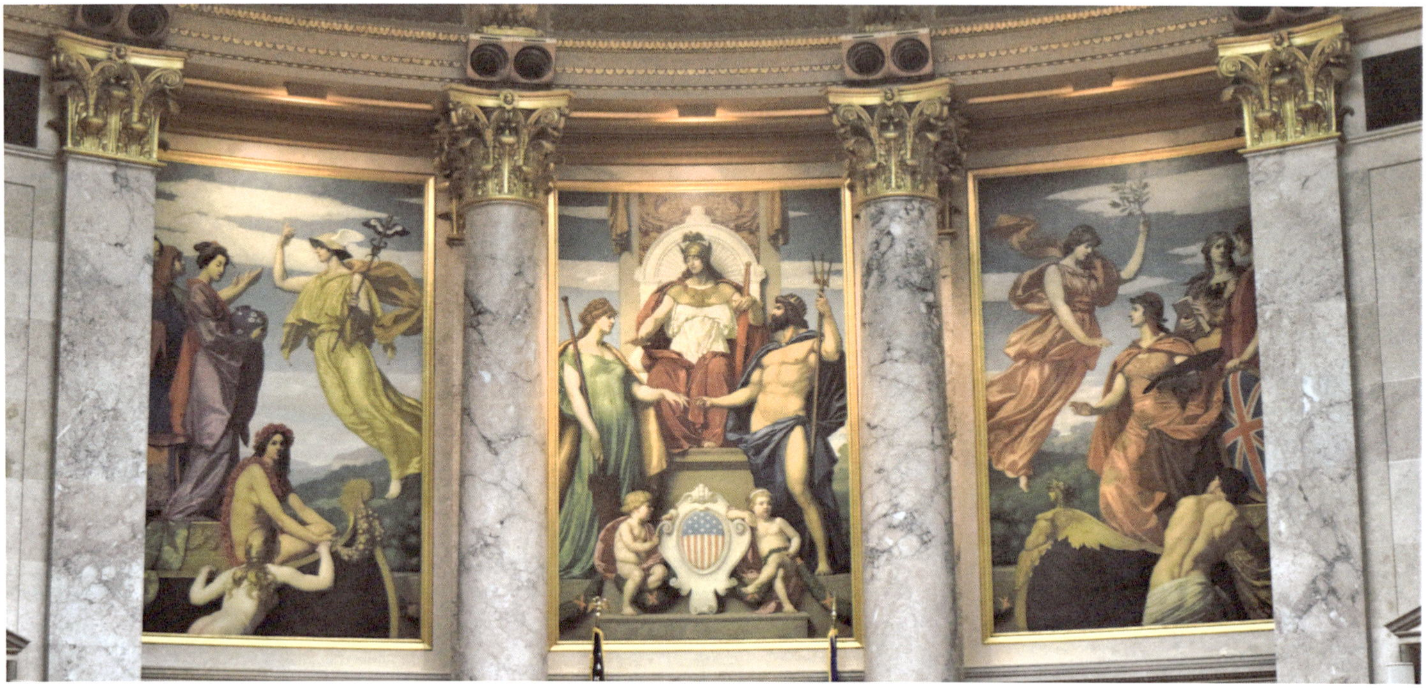

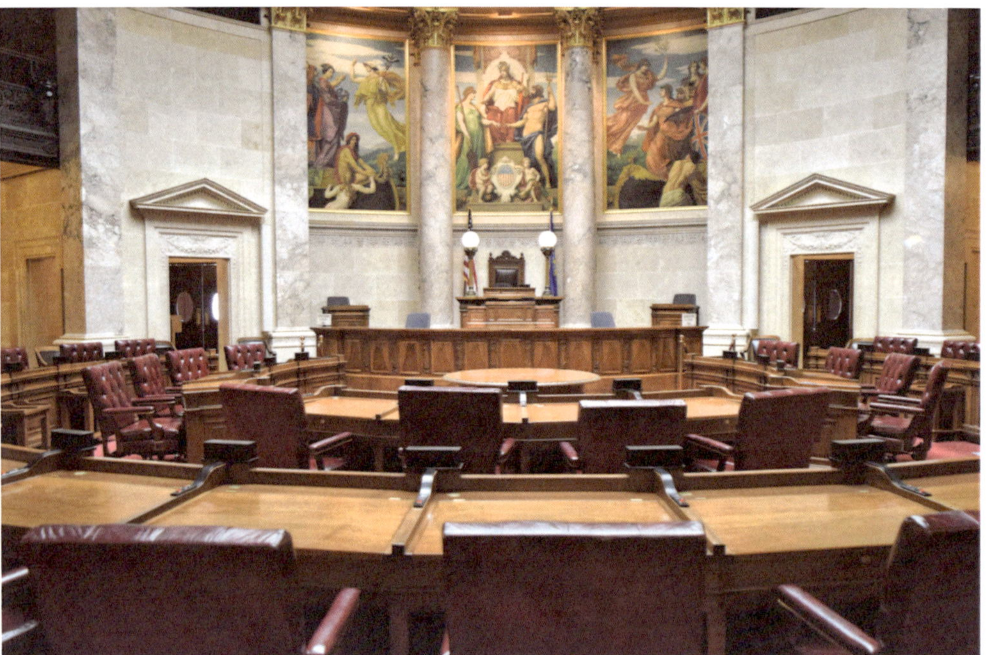

The Senate Chamber features French and Italian marble, walnut furniture, a colorful 30-foot skylight, and a Kenyon Cox mural "The Marriage of the Atlantic and Pacific.

These three separate paintings, collectively, symbolize the opening of the Panama Canal - with the Orient on the left and Europe on the right.

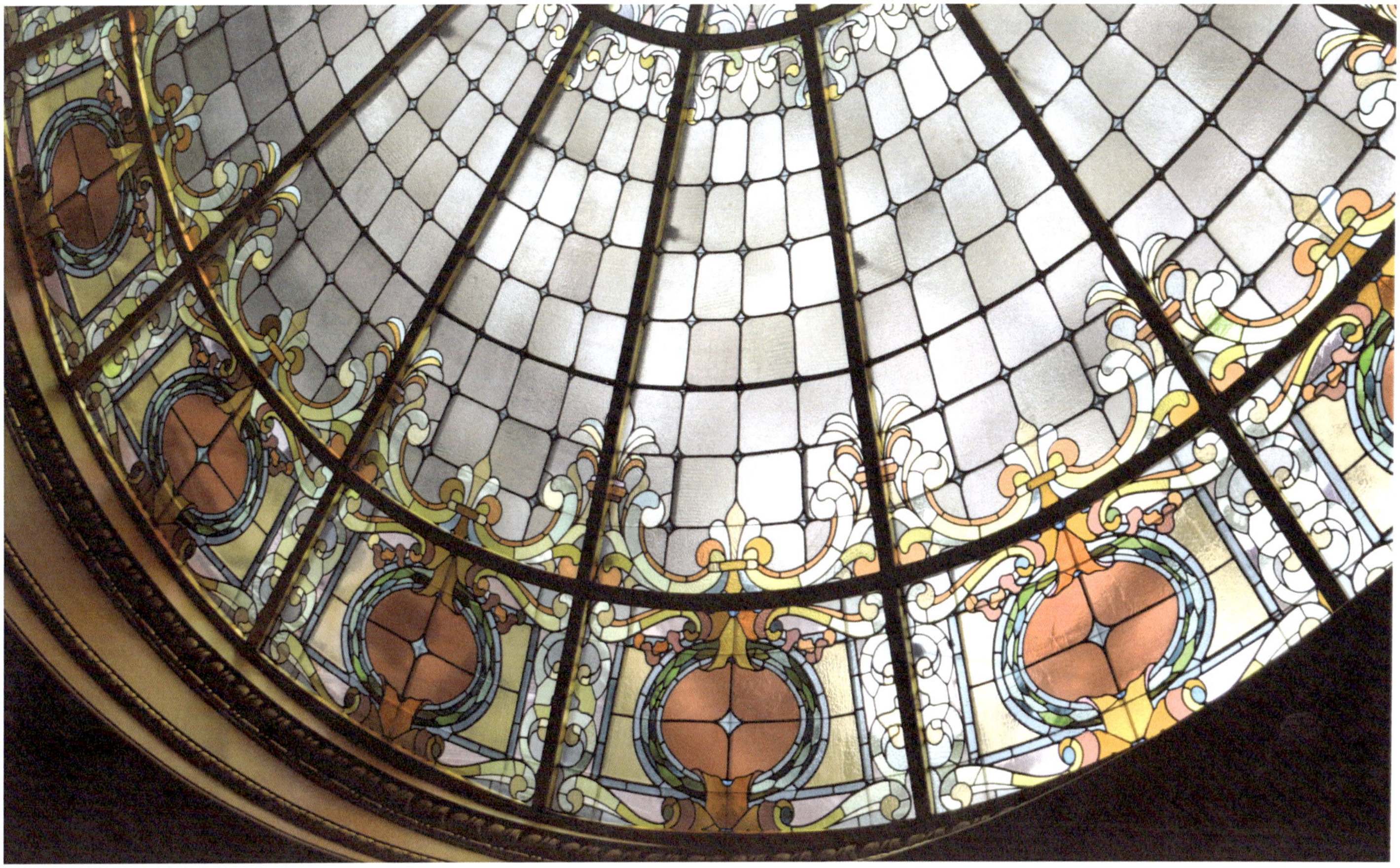

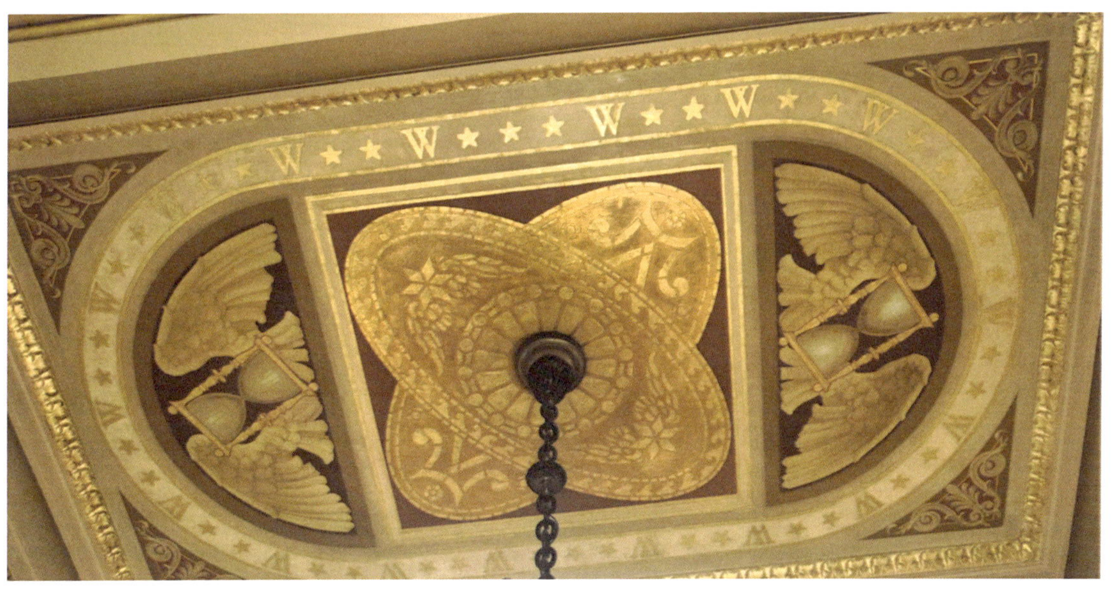

Old Abe' presides over Assembly Chamber

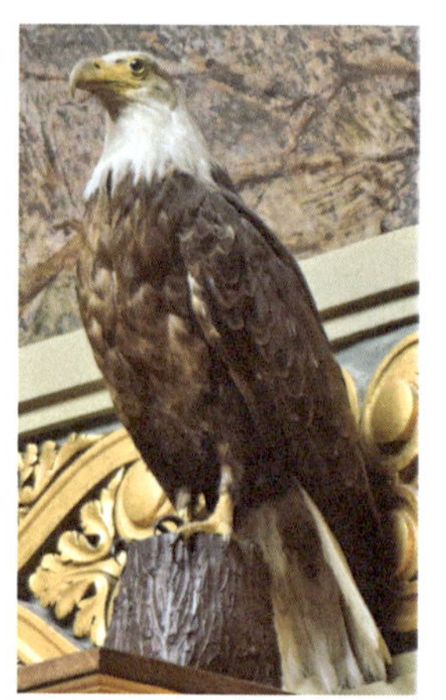

Old Abe a renowned Civil War veteran, this Bald Eagle has presided over the Wisconsin State Assembly since 1881. Old Abe rose to prominence during the Civil War as the mascot of the 8th Wisconsin Infantry Regiment, known as the Eagle Regiment. The unusual mascot was christened Old Abe, in honor of the 16th president.

After the war, Old Abe spent his days in an aviary at the Wisconsin capitol building. The original bird died after fumes from a 1881 fire near his cage. The bird was taxidermy and put on display in the capitol. A second fire in 1904 destroyed the original bird's remains. A 'body double' mounted remains of another Bald Eagle now perches high above the state's Assembly Chamber floor.

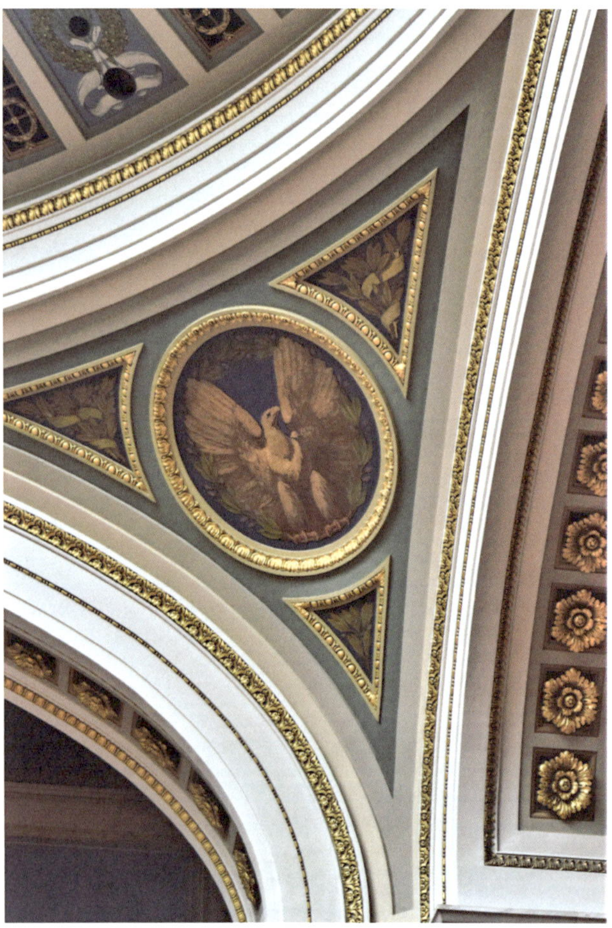

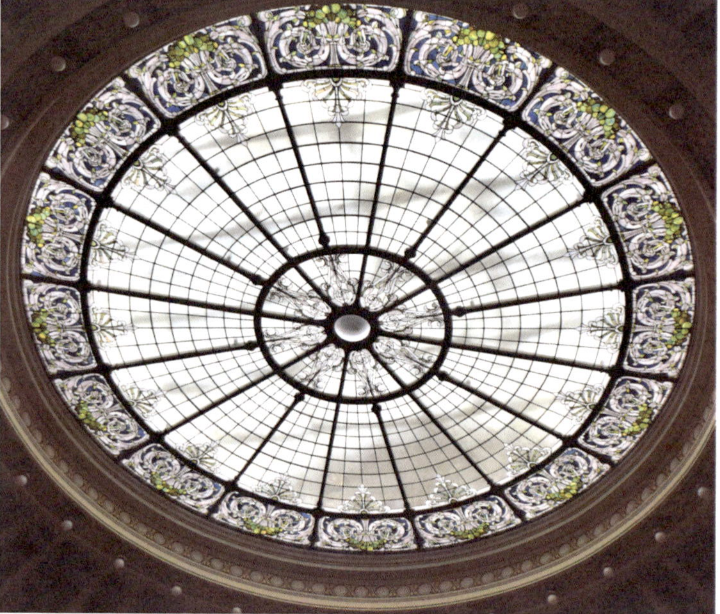

A 36-foot circular ceiling skylight of low toned leaded glass lights the chamber's walls of Dover marble from New York and the Italian marble columns.

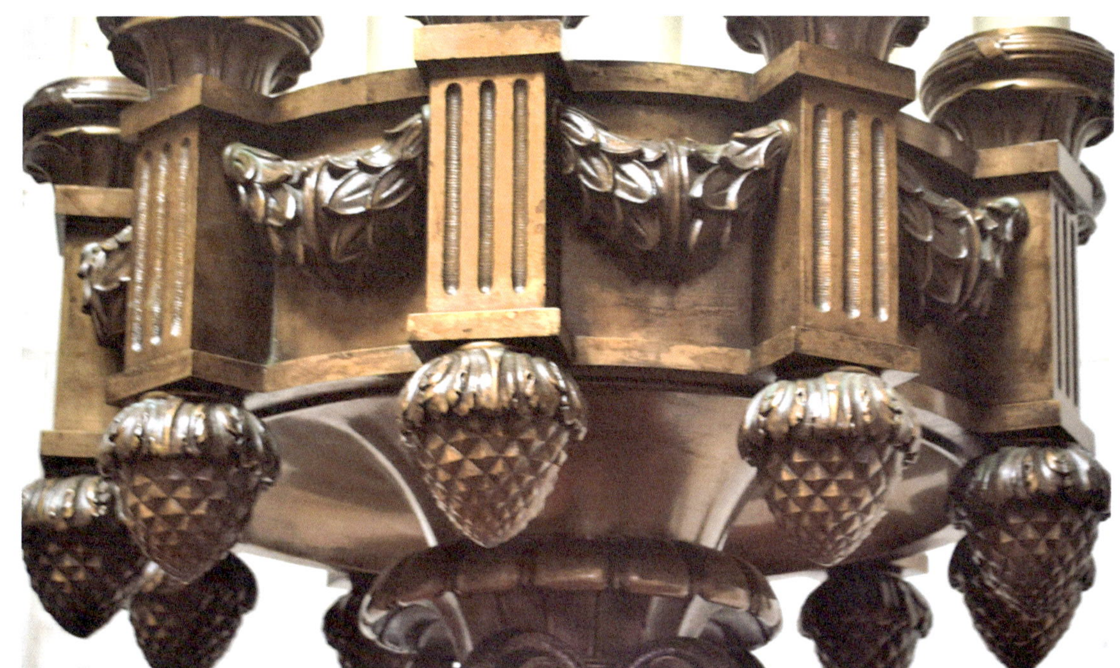

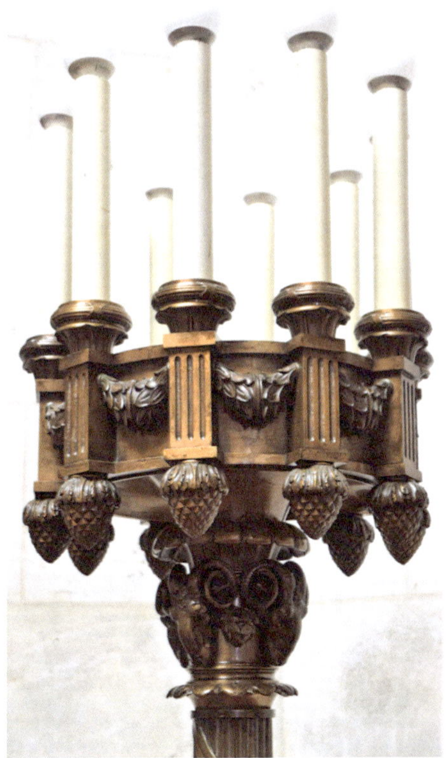

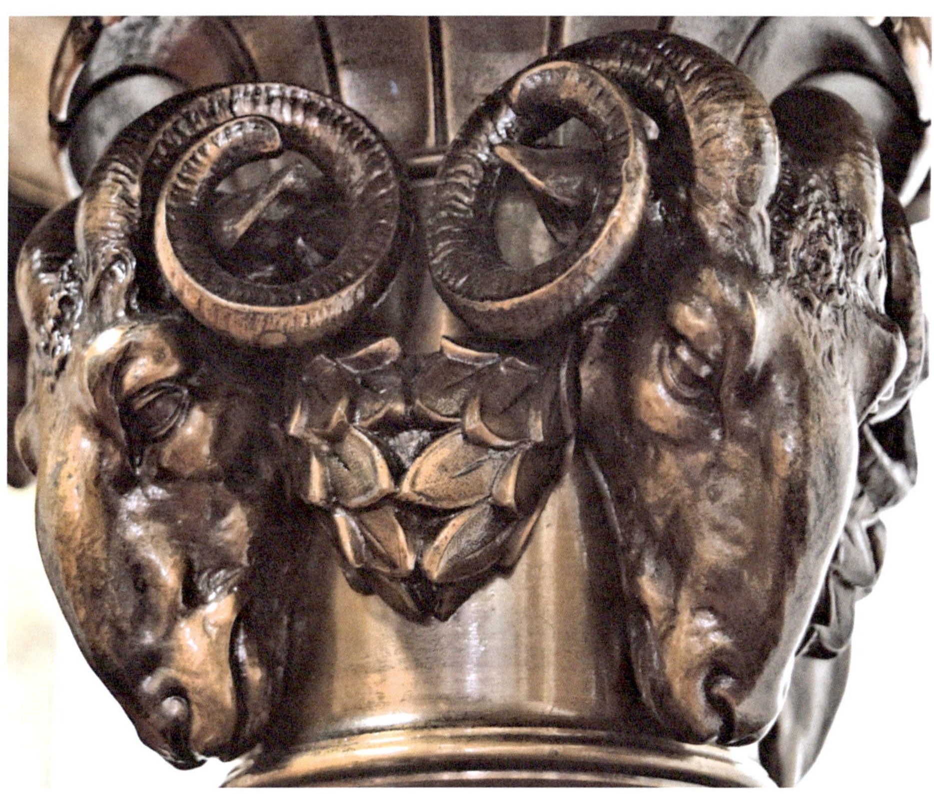

Governor's Conference Room

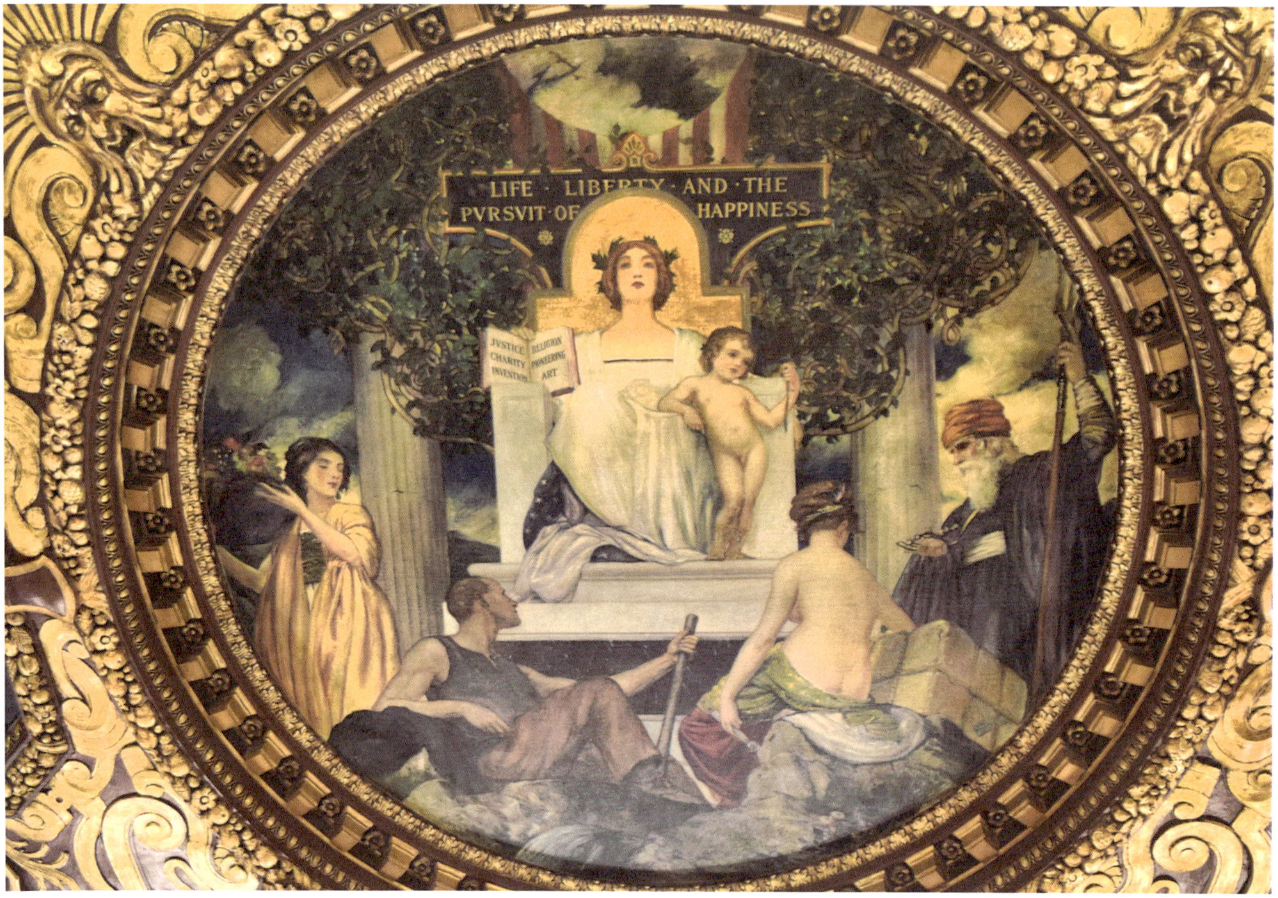

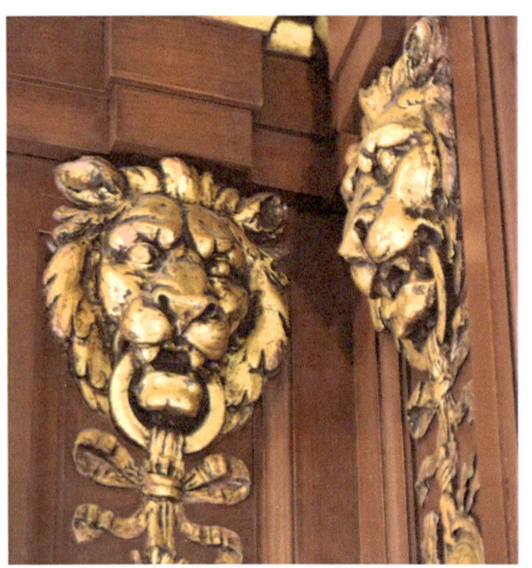

The Governor's Conference Room is styled after the small council chamber of the Doge's palace in Venice. The walls and ceiling are decorated with 26 historical and allegorical paintings by Hugo Ballin. The room features French walnut furniture and a hard wood parquet floor.

Renovations completed in 2002 returned the room to its original appearance. Remodeling in the 1960s and 70s had covered the gold and maroon walls with white paint.

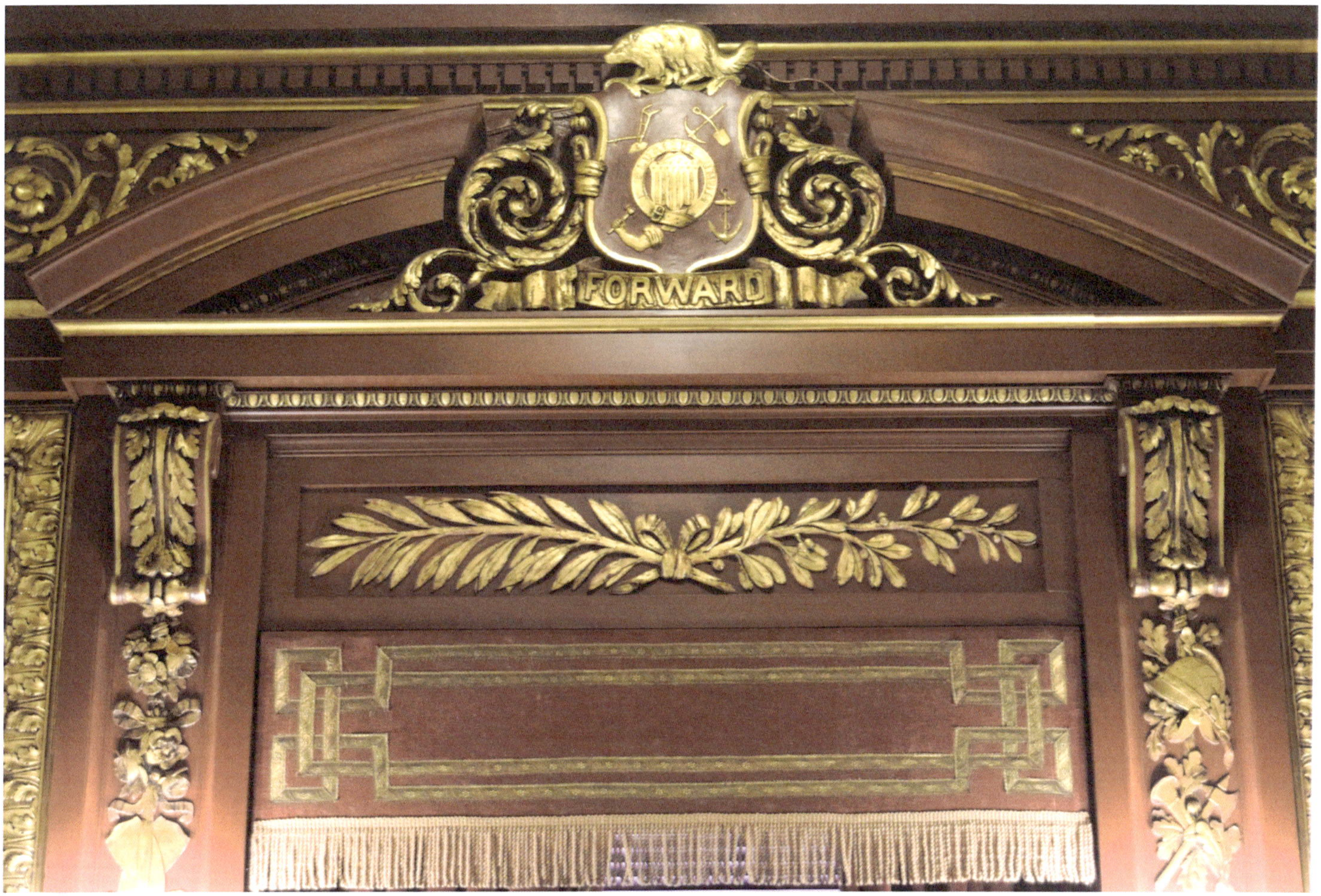

FORWARD

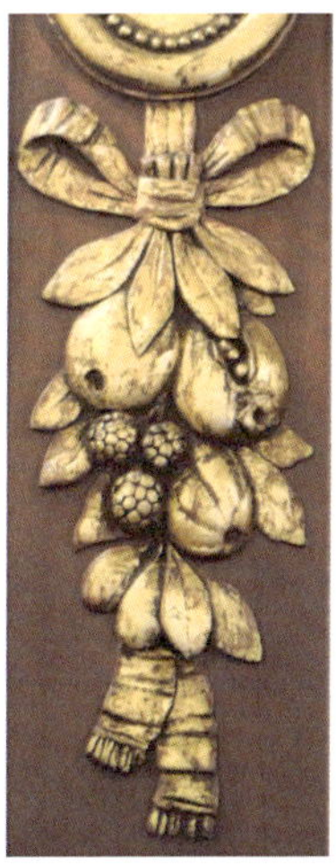

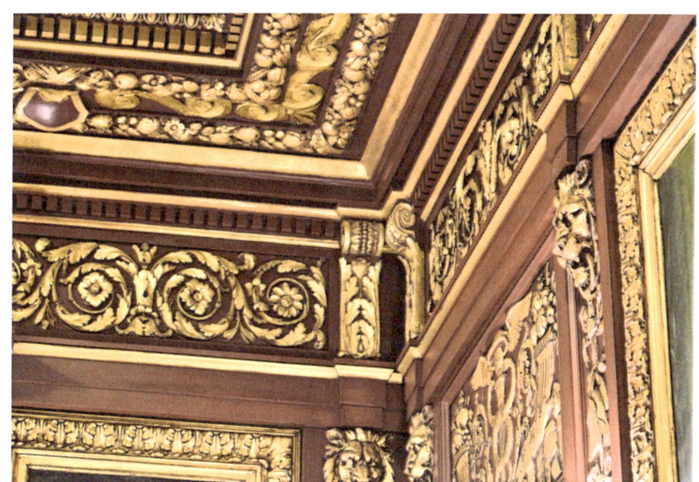

Capitol Sculptures

Each of the four wings of the building are fronted by a pediment with figures relate to the principle activities that occur within the building. The east wing, housing the Supreme Court, features a pediment by Bitter entitled Law; the south has Adolph Alexander Weinman's Virtues and Traits of Character, for the wing containing the State Senate.

Bitter's other pediment, the west, is Agriculture, while Attilio Piccirilli's Wisdom and Learning of the World adorns the north pediment. The carving of all these sculptures is attributed to the Piccirilli Brothers.

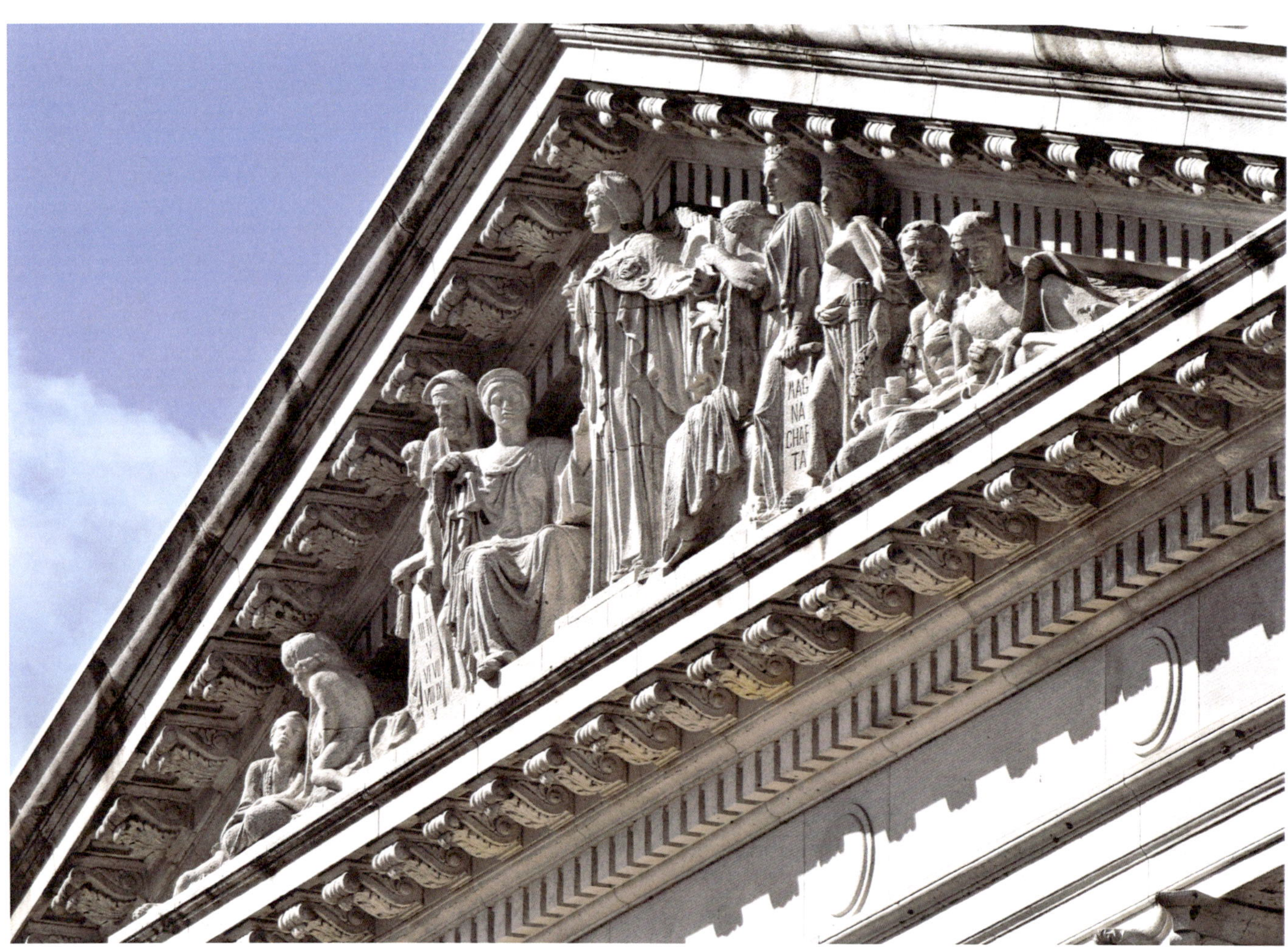

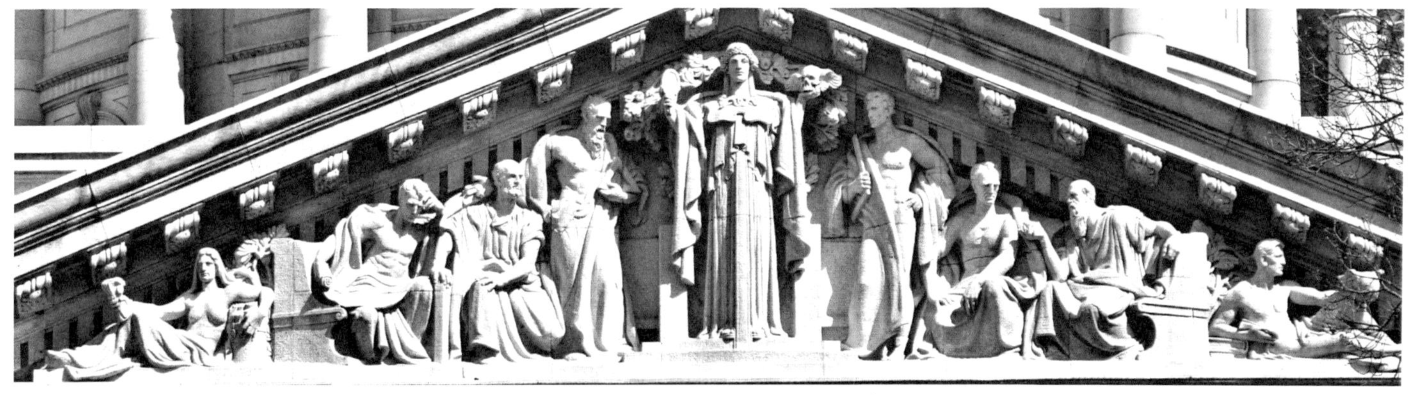

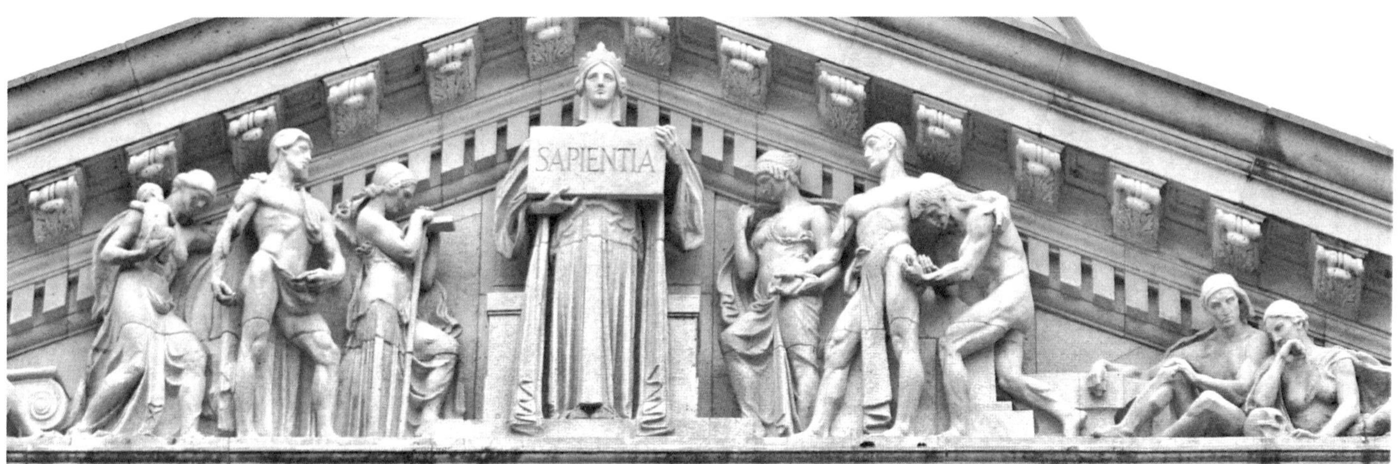
SAPIENTIA

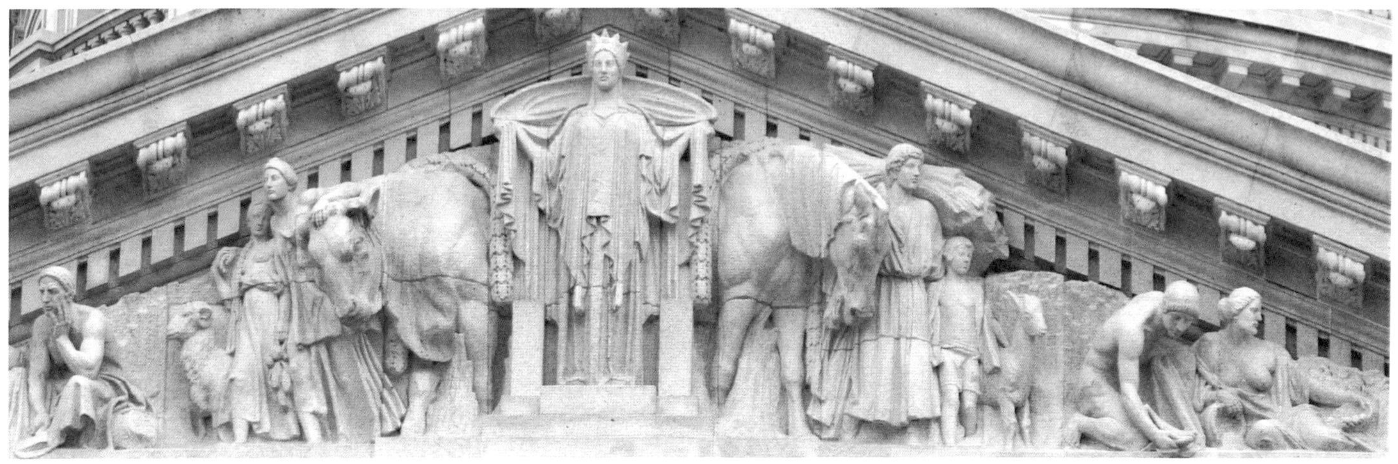

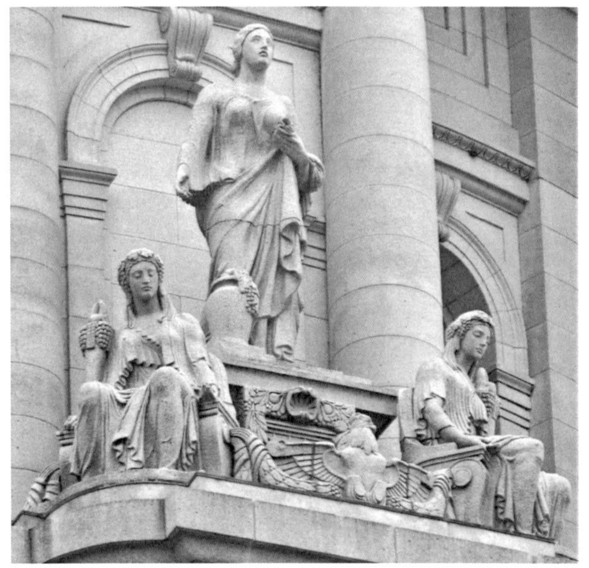
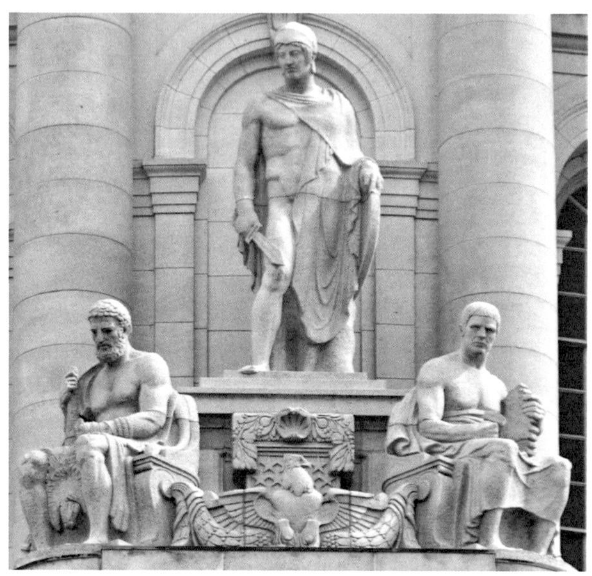
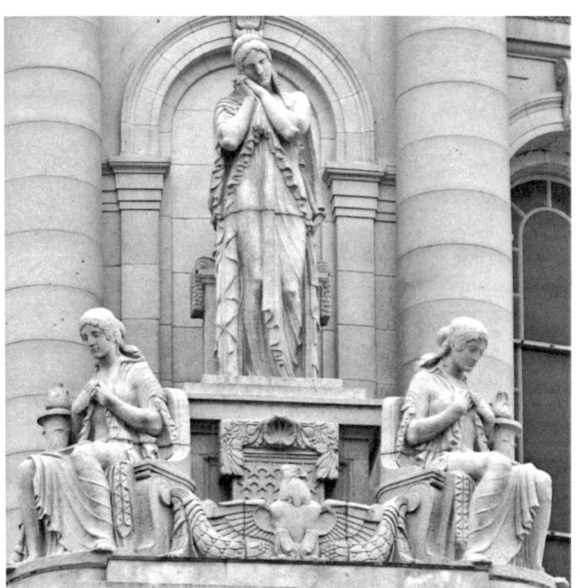
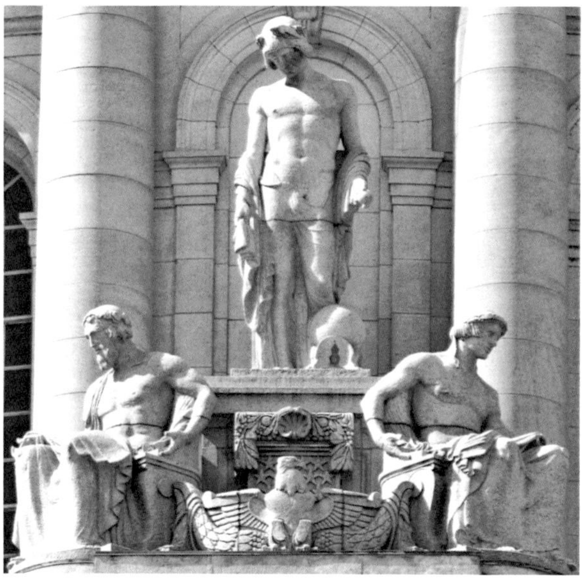

At the juncture of the building's four wings to the central section resides four sculpture groups by Karl Bitter. These groups, adorned in Greek clothing symbolize Faith, Strength, Prosperity and Abundance, and Knowledge.

Two additional statues on the capitol grounds are "Forward" by Jean Miner, and "Genius of Wisconsin," by Helen Mears.

"Forward, photo to right, is an allegorical bronze statue of a woman raising her right arm as a symbol of progress. Completed at the World Columbian Exposition of 1893 held in Chicago. After 80 years of weathering, the original statue was restored and placed inside the Wisconsin Historical Society building. A replica is now located in front of the west entrance.

"Genius of Wisconsin" is a statue of an allegorical woman in an embrace with an eagle, sheltering her head under its outstretched wings.

Mears originally created it in clay for the World Columbian Exposition of 1893 held in Chicago. and it was later carved in marble for permanent display in Wisconsin.

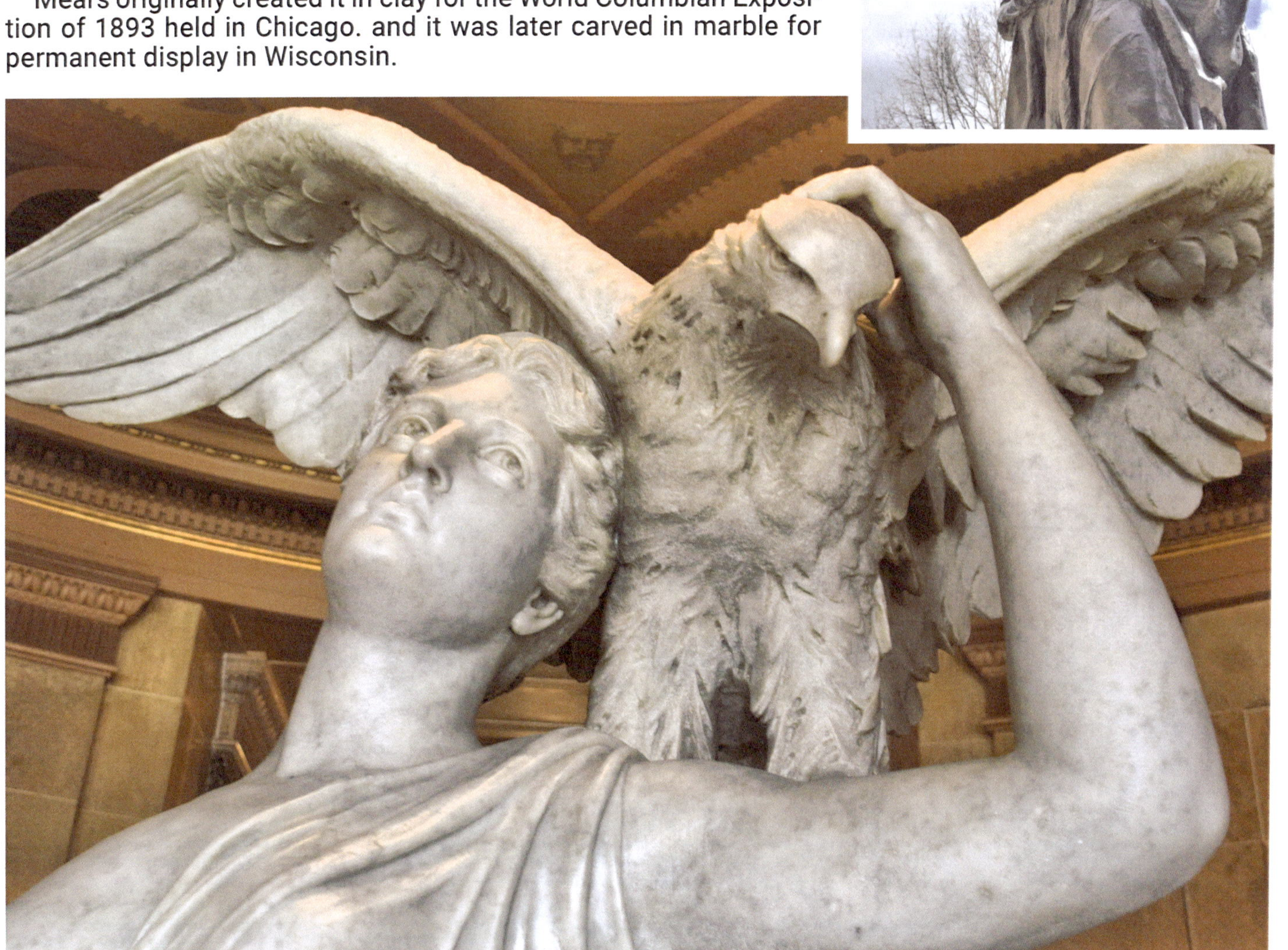

Wisconsin State Seal

The Great Seal of Wisconsin consists of the state coat of arms with the words "Great Seal of the State of Wisconsin above it and 13 stars, representing the original states below it.

Above the shield is the state motto "Forward" and a badger, the state animal.

Inside the shield surrounding a the U.S. coat of arms including the motto E pluribus unum is a plow, representing agriculture and farming; a pick and shovel, representing mining; an arm and hammer, representing manufacturing; and an anchor, representing navigation.

A sailor and a yeoman are at the side of the shield, representing labor on water and land.

Under the shield is a cornucopia, representing prosperity and abundance, and 13 lead ingots, representing mining wealth and the 13 original United States.

Various versions of the state seal are throughout the capitol, including, above, in the governor's conference room, and on door nob plates.

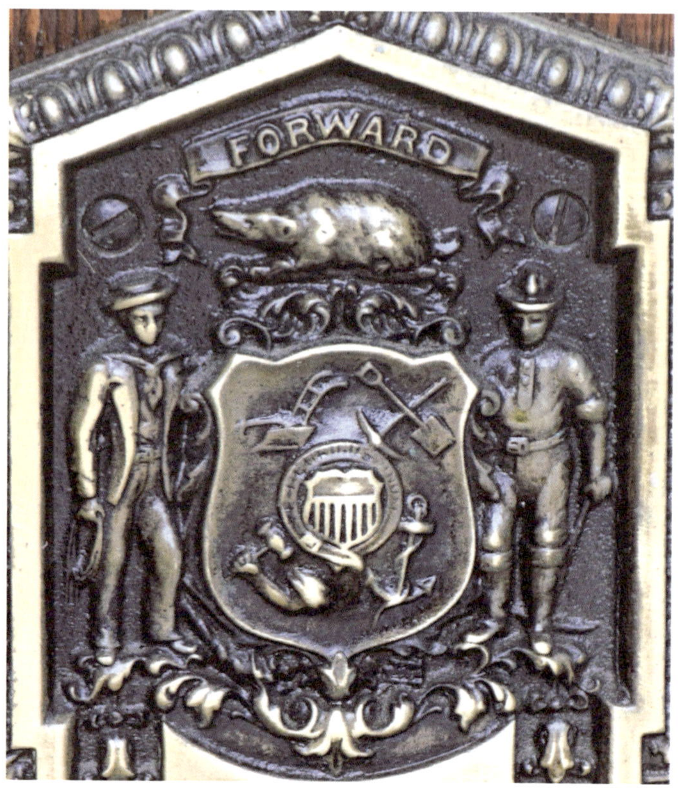

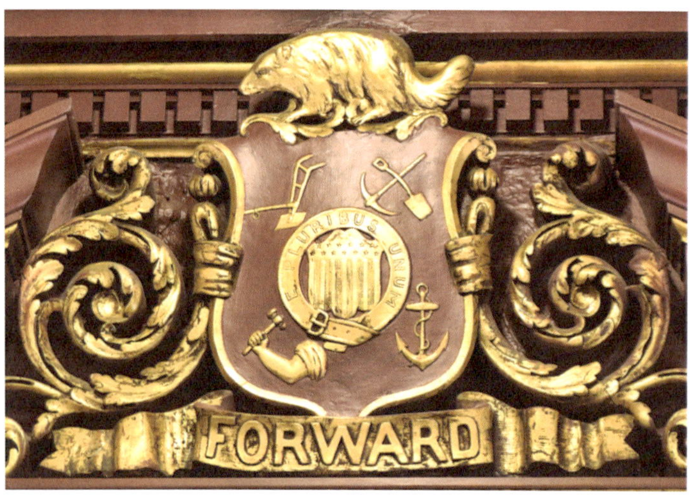

About the Photographer

Jane Moorman describes herself as an adventurer who loves to drive the backroads to see what there is to see.

During her 30-year journalism career, Jane honed her photographic skills as a photojournalist, including covering high school sporting events.

A friend once said, "I wish I could see the world as Jane sees it. Finding the beauty in things that most of us don't take time to see."

Upon retiring in 2021, Jane decided there is a lot of her native country she had not visited, including each state's capitol, so se began her journey of exploring the USA.

Jane currently lives in Albuquerque, New Mexico, but says her real home is on the road.